IMAGES
of America

THE LOCKHEED
PLANT

A Marietta-built B-47 Stratojet bomber roars off the Lockheed Plant runway in this early-1950s shot. The Stratojets were designed to deliver nuclear bombs. But because such bombs were so heavy and response time was at a premium in case the United States was attacked, B-47s also sported Jet-Assisted Take Off (JATO) rockets, as shown here, to get them airborne as quickly as possible.

ON THE COVER: What is now the Lockheed Plant in Marietta, Georgia, has produced many of the world's foremost aircraft since the days of World War II. And one of those planes, the C-130 Hercules, seen soaring over the plant in this shot from the early 1970s, has been rolling out the plant's doors continuously since 1955—one of only five planes in the world and the only military aircraft to be in constant production for more than half a century. At left end of the runway is Dobbins Air Reserve Base.

IMAGES
of America

THE LOCKHEED
PLANT

Joe Kirby

ARCADIA
PUBLISHING

Published by Arcadia Publishing
Charleston, South Carolina

Printed in the United States of America

Library of Congress Control Number: 2011925641

For all general information, please contact Arcadia Publishing:
Telephone 843-853-2070
Fax 843-853-0044
E-mail sales@arcadiapublishing.com
For customer service and orders:
Toll-Free 1-888-313-2665

Visit us on the Internet at www.arcadiapublishing.com

*To my wife, Fran, and children, Lucy and Miles, and
to the tens of thousands of men and women who have
labored through the years at the "Lockheed Plant"*

CONTENTS

ACKNOWLEDGMENTS

This book tells the story of what is commonly referred to as the "Lockheed Plant" in Marietta, Georgia, which has produced thousands of aircraft in the six decades since 1951. The earlier World War II operations of the plant were covered in my previous Arcadia book, *The Bell Bomber Plant.*

As with the Bell book, the telling of this story was made possible by the copious and, in many cases, compelling photographs snapped through the years by the plant's crack photographic staff. Most notably, John Rossino of Lockheed has chronicled every aspect of its operation since the early 1980s, and many of the photographs in this book were taken by him. Unless specified otherwise, all photographs were provided by Lockheed Martin.

My primary print sources of information for the text were the comprehensive *Cobb County, Georgia, and the Origins of the Suburban South* (2003), by Kennesaw State University history professor and oral historian of the Bell days Dr. Tom Scott; the highly entertaining and information-packed *Herk: Hero of the Skies* (2003), by retired Lockheed public relations executive Joe Dabney, which is the definitive history of the C-130 Hercules; and *Under One Roof: The Story of Air Force Plant 6* (2006), by Jeffrey L. Holland.

And Jeffrey Rhodes of Lockheed Martin's communications department is a walking, talking encyclopedia of knowledge about the plant and the planes manufactured there. Jeff, the associate editor of Lockheed Martin's *Code One* magazine, company historian, and the first to proofread this manuscript, graciously made himself available at all hours to answer my barrages of questions and, in nearly every case, had the answer at the tip of his tongue. If there are any errors in this book, they are mine, not his.

Thanks must go as well to Lockheed Martin vice president and plant general manager Shan Cooper for her enthusiastic support of the book and to company communications director Erica Crosling and communications representative Stephanie Stinn for their assistance early on. Lockheed Martin photographer Damien A. Guarnieri, with whom I've cowritten a pair of local history books for Arcadia's Then & Now series, went out of his way to try to bring new life to old photographs from the company's past. Retired Lockheed president Bob Ormsby was a big help as well.

Other thanks go to *Marietta Daily Journal* (MDJ) publisher Otis A. Brumby Jr. for graciously supporting the project and sharing photographs from the newspaper's files and to longtime MDJ associate editor Bill Kinney for sharing pictures from his personal collection. And a big thanks is due as well, and not for the first time, to MDJ newsroom assistant Damon Poirier for his support.

Lastly, apologies are in order to my wife and children for having monopolized our home computer late this winter in order to write this book.

To all, again, I give many thanks.

INTRODUCTION

The military and commercial aviation landscapes have changed tremendously since 1951. Back then, *stealthy* referred to burglars, not aircraft; cargo-hauling aircraft, as we know them today, were in their infancy, and *Hercules* was still just the name of a minor figure from Greek mythology. Moreover, there were more than 40 companies, large and small, designing and building airplanes in this country.

That slowly began to change that year, and helping to push those changes—and at the forefront of many of them—was the mammoth aircraft-building plant in Marietta, Georgia. In 2011, the plant marked its 60th year under the operation of what is now the Lockheed Martin Corporation and is the subject of this book celebrating those years.

Most agree that the construction of that plant at the outset of World War II was the most significant Cobb County event since the nearby Civil War battle of Kennesaw Mountain in 1864. In fact, many might suggest no other event has had an equal impact since the arrival of white settlers in the 1830s. Its opening was the key event in Cobb's transformation from the cotton-based economy of the Depression and earlier to the diverse dynamo it has now become.

The plant was operated by Bell Aircraft during World War II and produced a flood of B-29 Superfortress bombers—668 of them—that helped turn the tide of the war in the Pacific. These planes were identical to the B-29s built, ironically enough, under license from Boeing by Martin Aircraft in Omaha, Nebraska, which were to drop the atomic bombs on Japan. Marietta's population doubled almost overnight, as the plant proved a magnet, as it still does, for workers from all over northwest Georgia and as far away as Tennessee and Alabama. Cotton was still king in Cobb in 1940, but by 1945, the foundation was solidly in place that still sets Cobb apart from most of its neighbors.

When ground was broken for it in March 1942, the plant was the biggest industrial facility ever built south of the Mason-Dixon Line. Even with the onslaught of auto factories that have sprung up all over the South, it retains that crown today, nearly seven decades later.

During the war, it was commonly referred to as the "Bell Bomber Plant." However, starting in 1951 and for the following six decades, it was known as the Lockheed Plant; but its actual name is Air Force Plant No. 6. It was not owned by Bell, and although Lockheed has purchased substantial acreage for additional facilities south of the runway, Uncle Sam owns the main portion of the factory's campus.

This book endeavors to tell the story of the plant during its years of operation by Lockheed and now Lockheed Martin. The story of its World War II years has already been told in my earlier book for Arcadia, *The Bell Bomber Plant*, to which this book becomes a sequel.

It is not a strictly chronological history. There have been six types of airplanes built in large quantities at the plant and three other types in smaller numbers. In addition, there have been four major aircraft modification programs—to say nothing of the constant upgrades to the C-130 Hercules. And at frequent times, there have been more than one type of plane being assembled or modified, which translates to the kind of constant overlapping that helps the corporate bottom line but can drive amateur historians like this writer crazy trying to keep track of.

One other point should be made about this book. It does not try to adhere to all six changes in its name and Lockheed's corporate structure that took place through the years. It refers to the company simply as "Lockheed" from 1951 until its 1995 "merger of equals" with the Martin Marietta Corporation, which resulted in Lockheed Martin Aeronautical Systems Company, known today as Lockheed Martin Aeronautics Company. For simplicity's sake, the post-merger company is referred to in this book simply as "Lockheed Martin."

The Bell plant was completely shut down weeks after the surrender in Tokyo Bay and was used as a storage facility for industrial equipment, with only a skeleton workforce. The outbreak of the Korean War changed that in a hurry. The Pentagon decided it needed more B-29s and leased the plant to Lockheed so that it could refurbish 120 of those bombers, which had been mothballed in the Texas desert after the end of World War II. Workers at the plant were also soon producing hundreds of the new B-47 Stratojet, the jet-powered successor to the B-29, under license to Boeing. The Air Force lengthened the runway at the plant to 10,000 feet to accommodate the new jet. The runway was and is shared with what is now Dobbins Air Reserve Base on its east end and was shared for decades with Naval Air Station Atlanta, which is now closed, on its south side.

Meanwhile, Air Force brass had learned the hard way during the famed Berlin Airlift (1948–1949) and then again during the early months of the Korean War that its fleet of cargo planes was totally inadequate for the tasks at hand. They were based on civilian designs, meaning their access doors were high off the ground and were on the sides of the fuselage. In addition, the floors on some aircraft sloped toward the tail, and they were not powerful enough to lift many tons of cargo at a time. It was impossible to rapidly transport the heavy equipment—including tanks, trucks, jeeps, and artillery—a modern army needed moved.

The answer lay in a plane designed at Lockheed headquarters in Burbank, California. It was first flown on August 24, 1954, and was to have a huge impact on the company's plant in Marietta. The Air Force was looking for a plane that could do almost everything and found this ability in Lockheed's new plane, which was dubbed the C-130 Hercules.

Admittedly, it was not much to look at—chunky, pug-nosed, and without the streamlined beauty of most of that era's planes. In fact, Lockheed's design guru at its legendary yet secretive Skunk Works development facility in Burbank, Clarence "Kelly" Johnson, thought so little of the design that he almost refused to sign off on the proposal the company submitted to the Air Force for the right to build it.

Another of Lockheed's designers, Willis Hawkins, predicted the winning plane would be one that was a hybrid of a jeep, truck, and airplane. And that is as good a description of "the Herk" as any. It was a strategic four-engine airlifter with the endurance to cross oceans, to carry 90 soldiers for 2,000 miles at a stretch, to take off and land on short, dirt, or sand airstrips if necessary, to haul 30,000 pounds of heavy equipment in its boxcar-sized hold, and to slow its speed to 125 knots to let paratroopers jump. It would still be flyable even if it lost one of its engines. And it boasted a rear door and a cargo floor at the level of standard truck beds for easy loading.

Lockheed won the contract and later decided to build the C-130 at the plant in Marietta in the B-1 Building, which boasts 76 acres of floor space.

The first Marietta-built Herk rolled out of the plant on March 10, 1955, and was flown 28 days later on April 7, with legendary Lockheed test pilot Leo Sullivan as copilot. Sullivan was instrumental in much of the Lockheed history in Marietta. The C-130 has been in continuous production at the plant ever since, giving it the distinction of being just the fifth airplane and only military aircraft in continuous production for more than a half century. Nearly 3,000 copies of the Herk have been produced since 1955, with no signs of diminishing demand for that workhorse.

In the 1940s and for years after, Marietta was known as the "Bomber City," thanks to the plant's efforts during World War II. It gained a new nickname, the "Airlift Capital of the World," in the 1960s and 1970s. Not only did the C-130 continue gaining in popularity and effectiveness, but the plant also was chosen to build two larger and more powerful cargo-haulers, the jet-powered C-141 StarLifter and the C-5 Galaxy; the latter is one of the biggest planes ever built.

The C-141 was especially significant on two counts. First of all, it was the first aircraft designed and engineered at the plant that actually went into production and was built there; no longer was Marietta just an assembly plant. Second, the advent of the C-141 marked the end of the plant's days as a segregated workplace. Lockheed, like Bell before it, had adhered to Georgia's Jim Crow customs at the plant. But both corporations had hired African Americans in large numbers to do more than just menial work, and a degree of informal integration was already taking place in the plant in the late 1950s. The plant had eliminated separate bathrooms, fountains, and cafeterias by 1961, but despite those actions, when the Kennedy administration awarded the billion-dollar C-141 program to Lockheed in March of that year, the NAACP and other civil rights groups demanded the contract be cancelled because most jobs there were still closed to blacks. After negotiations with the White House, Lockheed announced it would fully integrate the plant. It was the first major manufacturing plant in the South to do so, and hundreds of others soon followed its lead. In fact, the integration plan, known as the Plan for Progress, was a blueprint for integration at industrial sites throughout the country.

Fast-forwarding 40 years, and in a move that would have been inconceivable during those days, Lockheed Martin appointed an African American, Lee Rhyant, as vice president and plant general manager in 2000. And even more inconceivable back then, the company in 2011 named a woman—and a black woman at that—as vice president and plant manager; she is Shan Cooper, who is more than capable of building on the legacies of her 15 predecessors. The Marietta plant would not have been the success it has been had it not been blessed through the decades with visionary, dynamic leaders, including men like Jimmie Carmichael, Dick Pulver, Larry Kitchen, Bob Ormsby, Ken Cannestra, Micky Blackwell, and, perhaps the most important of all, Dan Haughton, who ran the plant during the key early years of the C-130 program and then became president of the Lockheed Corporation.

The Marietta plant has always been one of Cobb County's biggest employers and, until the past decade or so, was *the* biggest, even though employment waxed and waned depending on war or peace and the demand for its various aircraft. More than 28,000 people (37 percent of them women) worked there during World War II. Employment spiked again at 32,945 (its all-time high) in September 1969 when both the Vietnam War and the C-5 program were in full swing. Roads leading into and out of the plant were choked with vehicles for miles at every shift change, leading some to make cracks about "the Marietta 500," as if it were a stock-car race. As this book was written in the winter of 2011, employment stood at just under 8,300.

Thousands of bungalows and duplexes were erected within walking distance of the plant during World War II, followed further away by thousands of brick, ranch-style "Lockheed houses" during the 1950s and early 1960s, which were sold largely to plant workers. Workers today, as they have from the start, commute to the plant not just from nearby but from all over northwest Georgia and metro Atlanta, and some from even farther.

The plant's presence has had an equal impact on the local education establishment. The need for thousands of workers with the kind of better-than-average intelligence needed to assemble Lockheed's planes proved a continuing impetus for Cobb and Marietta schools to steadily improve. Moreover, the plant's presence here was a key reason behind the transfer to Marietta of what now is Southern Polytechnic State University and the beginnings of what now are Kennesaw State University and Chattahoochee Technical College.

In addition, the plant brought to Cobb thousands of engineers and managerial personnel from other parts of the country in its early decades, who helped give the community a more cosmopolitan, forward-looking outlook than most of its peers around the Southeast. That influx of Westerners and Northerners, many of them Republicans, steadily helped give rise to a true two-party system in Cobb County, which had been staunchly Democratic since Reconstruction.

The 1990s began with one of the brightest days in the plant's history—the announcement that it had been chosen to engineer and build the cutting-edge F-22 Raptor fighter jet, which even two decades later is considered the most dominant such plane ever built. The Air Force had planned to buy 750 of the Raptors, but due to the end of the Cold War and the plane's high cost (currently about $139 million each), Congress has steadily whittled the size of the Raptor fleet downward. Congress and the Pentagon now plan to buy just 187 and have essentially pulled the plug on the program.

But the plant is staying busy. It is building replacement wings for the P-3 Orion naval surveillance plane as well as the center fuselage on the new three-variant F-35 Lightning II, called the Joint Strike Fighter. It also is responsible for avionics and engine modifications for the Galaxy program, which aircraft are then designated as C-5M Super Galaxys. As of March 2011, four C-5s have now been upgraded to the C-5M model, with another 48 planned.

Since the mid-1990s, the Lockheed Martin plant has been producing the C-130J Super Hercules, an almost total upgrade of the original Hercules, with upgraded avionics, engine, and cargo-carrying capability and the ability to land on short, unprepared landing strips with a reduced number of aircrew members.

The C-130 has been put to an astounding number of uses, both military and civilian and by scores of countries through the years, and demand for it shows little sign of leveling off. Although the wisdom of some of the wars this country has fought in the past half century is open to question, what is not in dispute is that fact the fleets of cargo-carrying planes cranked out in those years at the Marietta plant have given the armed forces of this county an incomparable asset when it comes to fighting wars, waging peace, and carrying out humanitarian missions.

Hercules pilots have had a motto for years: "You call, we haul." But I would suggest that the motto is equally applicable to the StarLifter and Galaxy and exemplifies the confident, can-do atmosphere that prevails both at the plant and among those who fly the planes that are built there.

Bell, Lockheed, and now Lockheed Martin have proven that this plant has no peers in the aircraft-building business, whether talking about bombers, cargo-carriers, or fighter jets. It has been a remarkable 60 years for the plant under Lockheed's stewardship, with hopefully that many more to come.

One

EARLY BIRDS

Air Force Plant No. 6, which now houses Lockheed Martin, was built early in World War II. The Bell Aircraft Company operated the plant during that conflict and assembled a total of 668 B-29 Superfortress bombers, which were identical to those built by Martin in Omaha that were used to drop the atomic bombs on Japan. This is a war-era composite photograph of a B-29 and the new plant.

A surplus B-29 was donated to the City of Marietta after World War II and, sans propellers and armament, was transported to Larry Bell Park up Fairground Street from the plant. Partly obscured at the extreme right is the long flight of stairs used by residents of the Marietta Place apartments to walk to their jobs at the plant. The B-29 steadily deteriorated after being exposed to the elements and was sold for scrap after a few years.

Bell shut down the plant within weeks of V-J Day. It was operated with a skeleton crew of 80 workers by the Tumpane Company until early 1951 and was used as a storage facility for aircraft manufacturing equipment, much of it brought to Marietta from other factories around the country. The plant was reopened by Lockheed seven months after the outbreak of the Korean War in June 1950 to refurbish World War II–era B-29s.

The B-29s had been mothballed in the desert at Pyote, Texas. Lockheed sent a crew to fly the best back to Marietta. But the engines proved balky, resulting in several close calls and one crash landing. Eventually, Lockheed began removing the engines in Texas and replacing them with reliable engines for the flight. Then those temporary engines, seen here, would be removed and trucked back to Texas for a repeat of the cycle.

The Korean War was raging half a world away, and the World War II–era Bell Bomber Plant had just reopened in Marietta when this shot was snapped in May 1951 of the Cobb County Safety Parade. Lockheed's entry, bearing the motto "Lockheed For Leadership Safety Is Our Job," won first place that day for being the best float. In the distance is Cobb County's historic, steeple-topped courthouse, which was torn down in the late 1960s.

This was the second "all-hands" meeting after the plant reopened. The facility was still mostly filled with stored machinery, some of which can be seen in the distance. One of Lockheed's smartest initial decisions was to persuade popular former Bell plant manager James V. Carmichael, facing the crowd, to return as manager. As a teenager, South Cobb–native Carmichael was hit by a car and broke his back. He could only walk with the help of a cane, seen to his right. Carmichael had run for governor in 1946 as a progressive Democrat and came in first in the popular vote but lost in the primary to Eugene Talmadge, who won the county-unit vote. Carmichael then headed Scripto Inc. and built the Atlanta-based company into an international leader in making pens and pencils. When the Bell plant reopened, he was persuaded to take a one-year leave of absence from Scripto to help Lockheed restart the facility.

The first B-29, dubbed *Early Bird*, wings into Marietta from Texas on April 13, 1951. The Bell plant had employed 29,000 people during World War II and had offered previously unheard-of job opportunities for many residents and at good wages. The news that it was reopening was cause for celebration in Marietta.

One of the returning B-29s is reconditioned in the nearly empty plant in May 1951. The planes were washed, partly dismantled, and then reassembled. Parts were inspected, repaired, or replaced, and much of the electronic equipment was upgraded. So were the tires. This B-29 has only two of its six tires in this photograph. Much of the new workforce had been employed at the plant when the Superfortresses were assembled.

The first all-hands meeting took place in spring 1951 in the plant's main B-1 Building. By this time, B-29s were beginning to trickle in from Texas, and several can be seen behind the crowd. Plant employment, totaling 86 in February, had skyrocketed to 4,500 by August. The speaker is probably Lockheed assistant general manager Dan Haughton. The plant's reopening meant the prospect of well-paying jobs, and many who had worked there during World War II were happy to return.

Each B-29, and nearly all of the later aircraft built at the plant, contained more than a mile of wiring, much of it bundled into cables of up to 100 wires apiece. These women, seen here in 1953, are bundling cables. It was tedious work. Plant management assigned the job to women because their hands were considered smaller and more dexterous than those of men

These B-29s are further along in the refurbishment process and have been moved from the B-1 Building. The original plan in World War II was to paint the B-29s at the plant, but before that happened, it was decided to leave them in their natural metal state to save weight. All told, 120 Superfortresses were overhauled in the Marietta plant and redelivered to the Air Force in 1952.

Though many B-29s were mothballed between World War II and Korea, some were sent in that pre-satellite era for long-range weather-reconnaissance and photograph reconnaissance flights. Others were used to monitor airborne debris from aboveground nuclear weapons tests performed by the United States and the Soviet Union. This Superfort was photographed as it came in for a landing at the Lockheed-Dobbins runway.

A crowd of company and government officials gaze up at a new B-47 Stratojet bomber as it rolls out of the B-1 Building in 1953. By the later stages of the Korean War, it was obvious that the days of propeller-powered warplanes like the B-29 were fast drawing to a close. Lockheed management announced not long after the Marietta plant's reopening that it would begin manufacturing the Air Force's newest bomber, the jet-powered B-47. The sleek new bomber was designed by Boeing and was built under license in Marietta. Seen here is the sixth of the new bombers (a B-47B model) as it exits the plant. At far left, looking toward the camera, is plant manager and future company president Dan Haughton. At center, in a light-colored suit leaning on a cane, is legendary former Bell and Lockheed Plant manager Jimmie Carmichael.

Here, the B-1 floor is as choked with B-47s as it had been in World War II days with B-29s. In the foreground are Stratojets undergoing modifications, while behind is a parallel line of new Stratojets being assembled. Unlike the B-29 line, which exited the east end of the building, the B-47 lines were oriented toward its west end, like the C-5 Galaxy and F-22 Raptor lines in later years.

The B-1 main assembly building was big enough to accommodate two assembly lines for refurbishing the B-29 bombers and, later, for the B-47 bomber as well. Unlike automobile plants, airplanes are not assembled on conveyor belts. Smaller components were assembled along the outer edge of the factory floor and then gradually worked toward the ends, where the two main assembly lines ran out the facility doors. One of the nearly 3,000 B-47s upgraded in Marietta is in the foreground.

A technician checks the innards of a massive Kearney & Trecker (K&T) milling machine. When the plant was reopened in 1951, the floor first had to be cleared of the hundreds of machine tools stored there. Some had been "pickled" in oil to prevent rust, which meant they had to be cleaned before being put back in use or shipped to other plants.

A young woman, probably a plant courier, delivers what may be a set of work orders to the operator of this K&T milling machine. Despite the heavy industrial setting, neither seems to be wearing any protective gear. But that was par for the course in most factories during that era.

The B-47 was powered by six General Electric turbojets. In what was probably a staged publicity photograph, this picture appears to show a white worker and an African American on the same crew. The plant hired blacks in significant numbers for more than just menial jobs. But even though Lockheed was a California-based company, its Marietta plant adhered to the Jim Crow segregation laws then prevailing in the South.

This Stratojet is near completion in a nighttime shot snapped near the hangar door. The B-47s had a cruising speed of 557 miles per hour and a ceiling of 33,100 feet, with a combat radius of about 2,000 miles carrying a 20,000-pound bomb load. The B-47 was designed to carry atomic bombs and was the first US bomber featuring a swept-wing design to be produced in large numbers.

The B-47 boasted an enormous fuel capacity of 17,000 gallons, more than triple that of the B-29. Some Stratojets also featured external drop tanks with a capacity of 1,780 gallons. But the Air Force wanted the aircraft to have intercontinental range, and so it was also fitted for in-flight refueling. At left on the tarmac is a Boeing KC-97 Stratofreighter aerial tanker.

At the rear is a B-47. At the right is the tail of a KC-97 Stratofreighter tanker, outfitted with a boom for refueling other planes. The KC-97s had two decks. The upper level could carry cargo, while the lower deck was fitted to carry fuel. The Stratofreighters used aviation-grade fuel to fly, but they carried 9,000 gallons of jet fuel to share with other planes.

The KC-97 Stratofreighter's B-29 heritage is obvious in this full-length shot. Close examination shows the refueling boom extending from its tail. In the foreground at right is the nose of a B-47. The C-97s were designed as cargo planes. Though they began to be phased out as tankers in the mid-1950s, some continued in service with the National Guard until the late 1970s.

A Stratojet is towed along the runway, with a fire truck following close behind. The Air Force had asked for delivery of the plant's first B-47 by February 1953. Its "Into the Blue in '52" program resulted in the first Stratojet flight by the end of 1952. Plant employment was around 25,000 in 1953, which represented approximately 40 percent of all manufacturing jobs in the metro Atlanta area.

The B-47 remained the Air Force's primary bomber through the mid- and late 1950s, when it began to be replaced by the B-52 Stratofortress. The Marietta plant had built 394 of the B-47s (at a cost to taxpayers of $1.9 million each, or $18.7 million in today's dollars) by the time the final one rolled out in December 1957. This Stratojet, the first Marietta-built aircraft, is seen over Stone Mountain.

Trees frame the parking lot outside the B-2 (management) Building the year the plant reopened in 1951. With World War II's gas and tire rationing a distant memory and with the 1947 demise of the Marietta-to-Atlanta interurban trolley line, most of the plant's burgeoning workforce now arrived by car.

Visitors to the plant arrived via this lobby until 2007. Newly remodeled in 1951, it featured a linoleum tile floor depiction of the company's logo (since removed); walls lined with photographs of Lockheed's newest planes, including the F-80 Shooting Star fighter and the Constellation passenger plane; and, typical of the era, numerous ashtrays for smokers.

Lockheed set up its first employment office in Head House 1, through which Bell workers had entered and left the plant each day. Lockheed had access to Bell's employment files, and many of the thousands who had worked there during World War II were soon back building planes. Some 2,000 applicants a week were processed through this office in the summer of 1951.

Not long after the old Bell plant reopened, Lockheed announced that it would soon begin building the Air Force's newest bomber, the B-47, at the facility. Seen here in 1951 are engineers—including a female, an unusual combination in that era—hard at work in the B-2 Building, most likely on some aspect of the B-47 or C-130.

Children and some "older children" get an up-close look into the cockpit of a Lockheed F-80 Shooting Star on this visitors' day in the early 1950s. The F-80 was the first American jet fighter to enter production. A mainstay of the Air Force, it saw heavy action early in the Korean War. Its inferiority to Soviet-built MiG-15s caused it to be shifted to ground attack missions rather than dogfighting.

Here, an aviation legend salutes two others. A Marietta-built Lockheed C-130 Hercules, one of the most long-lived and versatile aircraft ever built, flies over the memorial to the Wright brothers at Kitty Hawk, North Carolina, where man first achieved sustained and controlled flight. This photograph was taken in 1963, almost 60 years to the day after the Wrights first flew.

Two

THE "HERK"

The YC-130, seen here during its maiden flight, was designed from the onset to haul cargo. Prior to that, most cargo planes were modifications of passenger planes. They either had angled floors or doors high off the ground and were loaded from the side.

The C-130 is probably the most significant plane in the history of the Marietta plant, where all but the first two have been built. The two prototypes were assembled in Burbank, California, and the first flights took place in August 1954. This shot was taken of the YC-130 prototype just after landing at Edwards Air Force Base, California, after its first flight.

Lockheed's two YC-130 prototypes are seen here over the Antelope Valley in California. Early C-130s had a distinctive Roman-nosed shape that won them no plaudits from Clarence L. "Kelly" Johnson, Lockheed's design wizard. Later versions sported a nose with a mounted radar system, giving them their distinctive appearance. The radar gave rise to the term "Pinocchio nose."

Georgia's first C-130 was a full-sized, wooden mock-up weighing 100,000 pounds, seen here. It was shipped from California through the Panama Canal to Savannah and then brought to Marietta aboard a pair of tractor-trailers. Its arrival in Marietta was a big event in fall 1953, and its presence saved thousands of man-hours in engineering and manufacturing time.

This C-130, Company No. 3004, was one of the first built in Marietta. In the background can be seen the last of the B-47s, headed toward the exit door on the opposite end of the plant. The Korean War had proven the need for a better cargo plane. It had taken six weeks for the Air Force to transport two divisions to Korea by air when the war unexpectedly broke out. The existing planes could not lug tanks, trucks, artillery, or other heavy items.

The C-130 was the first American plane to feature turboprop engines, which use a jet engine to turn the propeller. That gave it tremendous power and fuel efficiency. The four turboprops on each of the early C-130s gave them a speed of 360 miles per hour, which was even faster than the passenger airliners of that era. Here, the first production C-130 is being towed out of the Marietta hangar in the rain.

Gov. Marvin Griffin did the honors at the rollout of the first C-130 at the plant on March 10, 1955, but it took him four tries to break the bottle of Chattahoochee River water on the plane's nose. "You build tough planes," the governor quipped.

Marietta's first C-130 Hercules takes off for the first time on April 7, 1955. As for the plane's name, a contest was held in 1954 that attracted almost 10,000 suggestions, the most common being *Griffin*—though that likely had more to do with the mythological creature than with the state's governor. Lockheed management chose instead to honor Hercules, strongman of Greek mythology. The name also kept the Lockheed tradition of naming aircraft after celestial bodies.

A crowd gathers after the initial test flight of the first Marietta-built C-130. The flight went extraordinarily well. But at the end of its third test flight a week later, this plane's engine caught fire. Luckily, the crew was fine. The Hercules was soon put back in service and, after being converted into a gunship, flew 4,500 hours of combat service during the Vietnam War. It was retired in 1995.

It was all smiles for the crew of the first production C-130 Hercules as it completed its test flight. In the doorway is test pilot Leo Sullivan, the most famous such pilot in Lockheed history. The crew consisted of flight engineer Chuck Littlejohn, pilot Bud Martin, Sullivan, and flight engineers Bob Brennan and Jack Gilley. Pilots through the years have uniformly agreed that the Herk is an easy plane to fly, especially for its size. One reason is the excellent visibility the design affords the pilots. Cockpits on early-model Herks featured 23 large windowpanes (now just 19 on the C-130J model), not only to the front and sides but on the lower sides of the cockpit as well. That comes in handy for pilots landing C-130s on rough landing strips. A half century after the first flight, the US Air Force chose its anniversary, April 7, as an appropriate day to receive the first of 14 updated C-130Js at the US base at Ramstein, in Germany, in 2009.

An early model C-130 flies high over the Lockheed Plant in this undated vintage picture. Just below the Herk's tail can be seen the Marietta Place apartments, hurriedly built during World War II to house workers at the Bell plant. At the left end of runway is Dobbins Air Reserve Base, and on the far side of the runway at right is the Naval Air Station Atlanta, which is now closed.

The first of nearly 3,000 C-130 Hercules built in Marietta is seen here rounding Stone Mountain during its first-ever flight. At the controls are test pilots Bud Martin in the pilot seat and Leo Sullivan as copilot. The legendary Sullivan was, over the next 40 years, the pilot in command for the first flights of Lockheed's XV-4, LASA-60 JetStar, C-141A, and C-5A.

Take that, Thunderbirds! These C-130A pilots at Ardmore Air Force Base in Oklahoma choreographed their own aerial acrobatics show in 1957, performing formation maneuvers with their wings just six feet apart. For nearly three years, the impromptu team, known as the Four Horsemen, was the world's only four-engine precision-flying team, wowing audiences around the world. From left to right are Capts. Gene Chaney, William Hatfield, James Akin, and David Moore.

Here, one can see a Hercules fuselage in mid-assembly. The Lockheed Plant has churned out more than 2,400 of the C-130 and its 70 variants. It is flown by the US Air Force, Air National Guard, Air Force Reserve, Marine Corps, Navy, and Coast Guard as well as more than 70 foreign air forces. Australia has flown C-130s for more than 50 years.

These Marietta-built C-130 Herks got a warm welcome, including a lei draped over the nose, when they stopped at Hickam Air Force Base in Hawaii as part of an eight-plane unit heading to the Far East to fly support for the Pacific Air Command in the late 1950s. The press release that accompanied the photograph noted that the plane was welcomed by a pair of "Chamber of Commerce representatives," presumably the young ladies in sarongs. In the above picture, they greet unit commander Lt. Col. Edwin Hibner. In the picture below, they find an admiring audience in the crewmen, who were midway through an 8,000-mile flight.

The Herk is the largest and heaviest aircraft to take off and land on an aircraft carrier. A Marine KC-130F, crewed by Lt. James Flatley III (USN) and Lt. Comdr. W.W. "Smokey" Stovall (USN), achieved the feat 21 times beginning on October 30, 1963, from the USS *Forrestal* while under way off Cape Cod. They also made 29 touch-and-go landings. Navy brass ultimately decided to use a smaller cargo plane on carriers.

The Royal Air Force (RAF) has been flying C-130Ks (actually a variant of the C-130H) since December 1966; although, the United Kingdom designates them as the Hercules C Mk 1. They also boast British communications and navigation equipment. The RAF's Herks saw service in the Falklands War in 1982. The RAF began replacing them with the upgraded C-130Js, known as Hercules C Mk 4 and Mk 5, in 2000.

The Hercules is more than just a military aircraft and has flown humanitarian missions almost from the very start, as seen in this 1966 photograph of a company-owned plane delivering supplies in Ethiopia. Often called the "Mercy Bird of the World," it is first on the scene after nearly every natural disaster anywhere in the world. C-130s from 14 countries were in Japan days after the devastating 2011 earthquake and tsunami.

The Hercules met the Air Force's criteria for a plane that could take off and land on short, dirt battlefront runways, carry 90 troops for 2,000 miles at a time, haul 30,000 pounds of equipment, drop paratroopers, evacuate casualties, and do so even with one of its engines out of commission. It is no wonder one of its designers said it would have to be part jeep, part truck, and part plane.

US troops wait to embark on a C-130 during the Vietnam War. A close examination shows the Hercules operating on an unpaved airfield. Early tests at Eglin Air Force Base in Florida showed a fully loaded C-130 could take off from dirt strips even though its tires had sunk more than 20 inches in the sandy soil.

The Hercules was a workhorse throughout the Vietnam War and proved especially invaluable during the successful months-long resupply effort for the besieged US outpost at Khe Sanh. Fire from enemy artillery and machine guns was sometimes so intense that C-130s unloaded as they rolled down the runway, then took off without ever stopping. One of the sayings of Herk pilots in those days was "You call, we haul."

With ground fire too hot to risk landing or a low-level drop, a C-130 dumps containers of supplies out its rear to embattled Marines below during the 1968 siege of Khe Sanh. By the end of 1967, the Air Force, spearheaded by the C-130s, had set a world record for the longest sustained airlift in history, longer even than that of the Berlin Airlift of 1948–1949.

These soldiers appear to have just exited a nearby C-130 in what likely was a "hot LZ," or landing zone, during the Vietnam War. The Hercules was designed to utilize "hastily prepared," which meant unpaved, runways that were under fire and to remain operational even if one of its four engines was lost to enemy fire. All told, 70 of the Herks were lost in Vietnam.

A Herk No. 3555 does a flyby down the runway in Marietta. In Vietnam, the Herks hauled in weapons, ammo, chow, mail, and men, despite being shot full of holes at times by enemy ground fire. On the way out, they could be reconfigured to medevac the casualties. When there was no room to land, the C-130s dropped in supplies by air. Others were specially modified for several missions, including serving as AC-130 gunships, wreaking havoc over the Ho Chi Minh Trail.

The C-130 has been put to good use by the Marines since 1960, making it the longest-serving aircraft in US Navy history. The Marines bought their first KC-130Fs in 1958 (with delivery in 1960) for use as aerial tankers. At that time as now, each KC-130 was equipped with a removable 3,600-gallon stainless steel fuel tank, carried in the cargo compartment.

The Marines call their KC-130s "BattleHerks." Here, in a picture from the 1980s, one can see a BattleHerk tanker refueling a pair of Marine CH-53 Sea Stallion helicopters, each carrying a Light Armored Vehicle in a sling load. Its ability to refuel choppers allowed the rescue version of the C-130, the HC-130, to fly into North Vietnam to recover downed US fliers during the Vietnam War.

Israeli commandos flew four C-130Hs more than 2,500 on the night of July 4, 1976, to successfully rescue 103 Jewish hostages being held by Palestinian terrorists and Ugandan dictator Idi Amin at Entebbe Airport in that Central African country. The hostages had been passengers on a hijacked Air France airliner and were only a few hours away from being executed when the Herks and commandos swooped in.

This C-130, known as *Fat Albert*, not only carries 40 and support personnel, parts, and equipment from show to show with the Blue Angels but is also an integral part of them. "Bert" begins his part of the show by firing Jet-Assisted Takeoff bottles—eight solid-fuel rockets (four on each side)—near the rear paratrooper doors. That extra lift lets the Hercules take off at a 45-degree angle and climb to 1,000 feet in just 15 seconds.

This is how the C-130 looked in "civvies," the L-100-30 civilian variant of the Hercules. The plane was developed after a 1959 request from Pan American for a passenger plane based on the C-130. The Marietta plant produced 114 L-100s, which were flown by domestic and international freight carriers and foreign air forces. This "stretched" version is 14 feet longer than the original L-100. Production ran from 1964 to 1992.

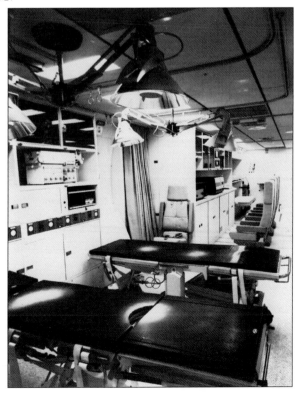

The Lockheed Plant configured 10 Herculeses as C-130HS flying hospitals in the early 1980s for Saudi Arabia. Each contained four hospital rooms equipped with an X-ray machine, defibrillator, blood bank, neonatal transporter, and more. Each also featured an operating room with a hydraulically operated surgical table, plus an anesthesia machine.

The US Coast Guard has flown C-130s since 1959 and uses them for long-range search and rescue, drug interdiction, illegal-immigrant patrols, homeland security, logistics, and tracking icebergs in the North Atlantic. As of 2011, the Coast Guard had six C-130Js in its air fleet, all based in Elizabeth City, North Carolina. Seen here are HC-130H model Herks at the Coast Guard airfield in Kodiak, Alaska, in 1984.

Some Herks were later modified into gunships like this AC-130H Spectre. They carried two 20-millimeter Vulcan cannons that could fire 2,000 rounds per minute—enough to cover every square inch of a football field in that time. Spectres mount a 105-millimeter howitzer so powerful that the plane fishtails in the air when it is fired. AC-130s are used for close air support, escorting convoys, and other missions.

A flight crew member looks into the dry bay No. 1 of a C-130 Hercules in this undated photograph from the late 1970s or early 1980s. The crew does not usually use low-tech means, like flashlights, to determine fuel levels, so this might have been a staged shot. The older Herks have four main fuel tanks in their wings, two auxiliary tanks, and two external tanks under the wings for a total fuel capacity of 9,530 gallons.

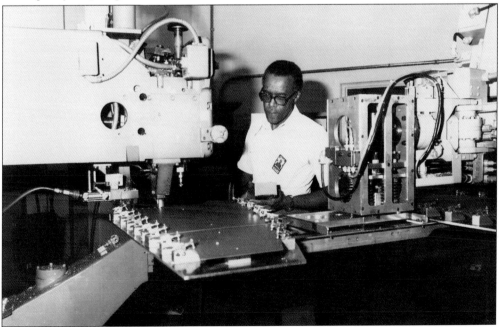

The Hercules was upgraded numerous times even before its groundbreaking J model was first flown in 1996. Lockheed made history in 1982 by being the first aviation company to assemble aircraft parts robotically. Here, one can see a plant worker using a robotic cell to assemble a cargo floor bulkhead web.

The Lockheed Plant for years employed a modified L-100-20 (the civilian Hercules) as the High Technology Test Bed (HTTB) aircraft to develop tactical transport technologies. The HTTB crashed just after takeoff from the Lockheed-Dobbins runway in April 1994, killing all seven Lockheed aircrew and flight test engineers on board. Seen exiting the HTTB in better days are, from left to right, test pilot Frank Hadden and crew members Kenny Rook, Malcolm Davis, Oakie Bankhead, and three unidentified individuals. Davis and Bankhead were killed in the later crash.

Niagara Falls is one of the few things capable of drowning out the drone of a C-130. Much of the sound produced by propellers is at very low frequencies, which travel further than other frequencies. Headphones are routinely worn by crews to protect their hearing and to be able to communicate. This C-130 was not the first or the last aircraft built at the Marietta plant to "pose" high over Niagara Falls. It is a tradition that began in the World War II years with a B-29 and has continued since then. Plant photographers also have captured dramatic photographs of Lockheed planes soaring over or past such landmarks as the Pyramids in Egypt, Mount Rainier, the Golden Gate Bridge, Georgia's Stone Mountain, and, of course, the plant itself.

Though the C-141 StarLifter was the first plane designed in Marietta to go into full production, the first one designed at the plant was the LASA-60, seen here. It was a light civil-utility aircraft that seated six people and was flown by the Mexican Air Force. Its first flight was in 1959. But only two were built in Marietta. Lockheed decided it would be unprofitable in this country, and so its production took place as a joint venture in Mexico as the Lockheed-Azcarate. Eighteen of the LASA-60s were built in 1960 and flown by the air forces of Mexico and five African countries—Central African Republic, Mauritania, Rhodesia (now Zimbabwe), South Africa, and Tunisia.

Three

JetStars and Other Stars

This Lockheed XV-4 Hummingbird was one of two built in Marietta for the Army and, later, the Air Force, in the early 1960s that took off and landed vertically, like a Harrier or the new F-35B Lighting II. The Hummingbird's performance was seriously lacking, however. Its top speed was slower than some propeller-powered transports. One aircraft crashed in Cobb County in June 1964, killing the test pilot. The second crashed in 1969, but the pilot survived.

This Marietta-built Lockheed JetStar served as Air Force One for every US president from Kennedy to Reagan. Pres. Lyndon B. Johnson was the most frequent JetStar flyer and often referred to the plane as "Air Force One-Half." The plant built 204 JetStar executive passenger jets between 1957 and 1978. Most were sold to commercial customers or individuals, including Bob Hope, billionaire Howard Hughes, and Elvis Presley.

Unlike many of the other planes built at the plant, the JetStar was designed primarily to haul people, not cargo. The later JetStar II aircraft were powered by four Garrett turbojets mounted on the rear of the fuselage and had a cruising speed of 504 miles per hour and a range of 2,995 miles. They were the first business-class jets produced in this country.

The JetStar was designed—back in the slide-rule days—by legendary Lockheed figure Kelly Johnson at the Skunk Works in California. He also designed the P-38 Lighting, P-80 Shooting Star, U-2 Dragon Lady, and the SR-71 Blackbird spy plane. This nearly complete JetStar II is the backdrop as Lockheed-Georgia president and plant manager Bob Ormsby (left) consults with an associate.

The first 16 JetStars were sold to the Air Force as the VC-140. The rest were sold to commercial customers. After a break in production for several years, Lockheed began producing upgraded JetStar IIs in the mid-1970s. The rollout for the JetStar IIs, seen here, took place in June 1976.

Here is an interior view of the JetStar II. Most of the JetStar IIs featured seating for eight with a full-sized restroom, although some were configured for 10 passengers. And it was one of the few executive jets with a cabin tall enough to allow passengers to walk upright. Designers made this possible by sinking the aisle slightly.

The JetStar II's sleek, needle-nosed good looks made it an easy sell to customers like Ford Motor Company and Corning Glass Works, as well as air forces in Germany, Mexico, and Indonesia. Its attractive appearance also won it prime movie roles as the personal aircraft of villain Auric Goldfinger in the 1964 James Bond movie of the same name and as personal transportation for John Wayne in *Hellfighters*.

The early 1990s saw the Navy and Air Force joining forces to develop a new trainer aircraft. Seven contractors responded to the request for proposals for the Joint Primary Aircraft Training System (JPATS), including Lockheed. The company partnered with Italian aircraft manufacturer Aermacchi and submitted an updated variant of that company's MB-339 trainer and light attack aircraft. It was called T-Bird II, seen here, in honor of the world's first jet trainer, the Lockheed T-33. The Aermacchi MB-339 T-Bird II had a 35-foot wingspan and was powered by a Rolls-Royce Viper turbojet, producing a top speed of 558 miles per hour at sea level. The two-seat plane had a range of 1,760 miles and a service ceiling of 48,000 feet. After a 14-month selection process, the Pentagon selected Beech Aircraft of Wichita to develop and deliver the JPATS trainers.

Though built a half-century ago, the XB-70 Valkyrie still looks futuristic. The Lockheed Plant made mid-fuselages for a pair of the experimental Mach 3 bombers for North American in 1961–1962 under a giant circus tent in the middle of the factory floor for extra secrecy. It never went into production, and one crashed after colliding with an F-104 during a photo shoot. The other is on display at Wright-Patterson Air Force Base, Ohio.

The S-3 Viking's first mission was tracking enemy submarines. During its career, it served a number of roles, including tanking. Known unofficially as "Hoovers" for the sound the engines make, the Viking first went into service in the early 1970s and was retired from Navy fleet service in 2009. Though the planes were not built in Marietta, the Lockheed Martin plant has been responsible for sustaining the S-3 since 1990 and maintains the handful of S-3s still flying today.

The first Marietta-built P-3 Orion maritime patrol plane soars over Georgia's famous Stone Mountain, with the massive carvings of mounted Confederate leaders visible just above the fuselage in 1995. P-3s first took part in the US blockade during the Cuban Missile Crisis and have been in continuous service since the early 1960s.

Like C-130s, Orions have a variety of uses, including hurricane reconnaissance, antipiracy patrols, homeland security, humanitarian relief, search and rescue, and intelligence gathering. Unlike the C-130s, the Orions' duties include antisubmarine warfare. US Customs and Border Protection aircraft were used for air traffic control over the 2010 Gulf of Mexico oil spill cleanup. They have cleared the airspace over the annual Super Bowl game since 2002.

Bob Ormsby, a Georgia Tech roommate of future president Jimmy Carter, headed Lockheed-Georgia from 1975 to 1984. His tenure coincided with the Air Force's decision to have the Marietta plant stretch each plane in its fleet of C-141s by 23 feet. Ormsby also was in charge when the plant won the contract to build 50 of the C-5B Galaxys.

Four

PLANT PEOPLE

The B-29s were part of the US Army Air Forces during World War II but became part of the Air Force upon its creation, as denoted on this plane's fuselage on the Lockheed-Dobbins runway. Posing for the picture appear to be some of the plant's engineering and/or managerial staff.

Cobb native Jimmie Carmichael managed the Bell plant during the war and ran unsuccessfully for governor in 1946. He took a leave of absence from the presidency of Scripto to serve as the first manager when Lockheed reopened the plant in 1951. Carmichael oversaw the B-29 modification program and planning for the B-47 before returning to Scripto in 1952. He served on the Lockheed board of directors until shortly before his death in 1972.

Dan Haughton succeeded Carmichael and successfully lobbied his corporate bosses in California for assembly of the C-130 to take place in Marietta. Haughton, who started with Lockheed as a systems analyst before World War II, later spent seven years as president of the company, followed by nine years as chairman of the board, overseeing development of the U-2 and SR-71 Blackbird spy planes and the C-5 Galaxy.

The first task for the new plant was to
recondition 130 World War II–era B-29s for
the Korean War. They had been mothballed
in desolate Pyote, Texas. Sherman Martin,
seen here in the 1980s, headed the team
that chose the best of them to be flown
back to Marietta. But the engines proved
so unreliable after the years in the desert
that Lockheed began shipping them to
Marietta separately. "Slave" engines were
attached so the planes could be flown back.

Four-star Gen. Howell Estes, seen
while visiting Lockheed, was born
in Fort Oglethorpe, Georgia, and
graduated from West Point in 1936.
He began his Army career riding
with the 7th Cavalry and later flew
25 combat missions over Korea in
B-29 bombers. Estes headed Military
Airlift Command from 1964 to 1969
during the height of the Vietnam
War, overseeing Lockheed-built
C-130s and C-141s. After retiring,
he was president of Federal Express.

Bob Hill of Marietta, here looking perplexed alongside an early-model C-130 Hercules, spent 55 years working for Lockheed and ultimately served as chief production test pilot, conducting test flights for the planes that rolled off the Marietta plant's production line. He was inspired to become a pilot when, as a boy, he would see B-29 Superfortress bombers take off from the nearby Bell plant.

Hill, age 77 as this book was written in 2011 and seen here by the props of a C-130J, retired in 2007 after having logged 14,000 hours flying for the company and having flown to 72 nations, which is a lot for a non-airline pilot. His son Doug is also a longtime Lockheed Martin employee. Working at the plant has been a multigenerational experience for many families.

Larry Kitchen, seen here at the JetStar II rollout in 1976, served as president of Lockheed-Georgia from 1971 to 1975, which were difficult years for Lockheed. During his later tenure as Lockheed board chairman and chief executive officer (through 1988), the company began moving heavily into manufacturing space and missile technology and products. (*Marietta Daily Journal* photograph.)

Lockheed-Georgia president Bob Ormsby, at the podium, delivers the annual Christmastime address to employees (note the wreath and trimming) in 1981. Behind him are the nose and fuselage of a C-141 being modified. Ormsby headed the initial design team for the C-5A Galaxy. Production began on the Galaxy in 1965, and the first copy rolled out of the plant on March 2, 1968.

Dan Haughton joined Lockheed in 1937. After managing the Marietta plant as vice president from 1952 to 1956, getting the B-47 and C-130 programs off the ground, he was promoted to president of the Lockheed Corporation. But he remained a frequent, and hands-on, presence at the Marietta plant, where he knew hundreds of employees by name. Here, the plant's flag flies at half-mast following his death in 1987.

Leo Sullivan was already famous within Lockheed ranks when he arrived in Marietta in 1952, after serving as a naval aviator and test pilot during World War II and then as Lockheed test pilot for the P2V Neptune, Constellation, and F-80/F-94/T-33 series. His legend continued to grow as he was copilot on the inaugural flight of the Marietta plant's first production C-130 in 1955 as well as the initial flights of the plant's XV-4 Hummingbird vertical take-off jet, LASA-60 single-engine plane, C-141, and C-5A.

Charlie Ferguson (right) was a Marietta native hired in 1951 to work on the building and grounds crew, one of relatively few positions open at the time to black workers. By the time he retired, he had worked himself up to a supervisory position on the C-130 assembly line. He is seen here in the 1980s receiving an award from vice president of finance J. Mark Chamberlain.

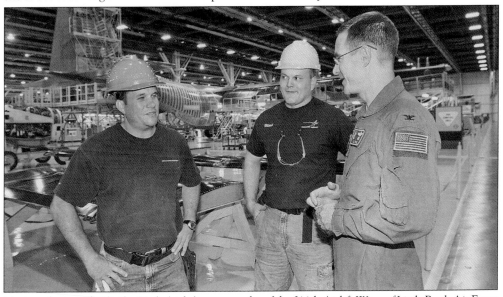

Marietta-born Col. Charles Hyde (right), commander of the 314th Airlift Wing of Little Rock Air Force Base in Little Rock, Arkansas, which flies the C-130, toured the C-130J production line in August 2009. Also pictured are lead mechanic Gary Byler (left) and mechanic Mitch Hendrickson.

When the 40th anniversary of the reopening of the plant by the Lockheed Aircraft Company rolled around in 1991, there were still 172 employees, seen here, who had been on the payroll ever since 1951. Eight of them were still working there on the 50th anniversary in 2001, and two were still employed as this book was being prepared in 2011—although, one of them was said to be "thinking about" retirement.

Lockheed stepped up with a $20,000 donation to the South Cobb High School marching band in January 2009, helping fund its trip to Washington, DC, to take part in the inaugural parade for Pres. Barack Obama. At far the right is Lockheed Martin vice president and Marietta site general manager Lee Rhyant.

This was the last Hercules to be flown out of Saigon at the conclusion of the Vietnam War. It did so with a record 452 men, women, and children squeezed aboard, including 38 squished into the flight deck alongside the pilot. The C-130 was designed to carry only 90 passengers and barely made it off the runway. It is now on display at Little Rock Air Force Base in Arkansas. Among those on that flight was Vietnamese air force officer Tim Nguyen. As he landed in Thailand, he vowed to someday work for the company that made the plane. He came to the United States as a refugee, learned English, earned a degree in electrical engineering from the University of Alabama, went to work at the Lockheed Plant in Marietta as a C-130 survivability engineer, and was named its Hercules Employee of the Year in 1992.

This C-141 StarLifter is being loaded, as is another in distance. Note the C-141's distinctive "clamshell" tail doors. As the 1960s dawned, the Marietta plant was chosen to design, engineer, and build a jet-powered transport plane that would be bigger, faster, and stronger than the Hercules. That plane was the StarLifter. And before the decade was out, the plant was chosen to design and build a cargo jet that was even bigger yet, one of the largest planes ever built, the C-5 Galaxy. All three planes would perform heroically in the Vietnam War and the wars that followed. And the StarLifter contract was crucial in another way for the plant as well, by leading to Lockheed's decision to fully integrate its workforce there—the first major industrial plant in the South to do so.

Five

AIRLIFT CAPITAL
OF THE WORLD

The rollout of the C-141 took place August 22, 1963, when President Kennedy pushed a button in the White House that caused the giant hangar doors of the B-1 Building to open. No prototype was built of the C-141. Every plane that came off the production line was put into regular service, including the eight that had been flown as test aircraft.

The C-141 had a range of just less than 3,000 miles fully loaded and four Pratt & Whitney engines, which produced speeds up to 567 miles per hour. But perhaps its greatest significance to Georgia was that it was the first Lockheed production aircraft designed and built from the start at the Marietta plant. Production began in May 1962 and peaked in 1967, when 107 of the jets rolled out.

Production began on the C-141 in May 1962 and peaked in 1967, when 107 of the jets rolled out. Most were soon pressed into service flying men and supplies to Vietnam. Four decades later, some of them were flying wounded servicemen back from the Persian Gulf or suspected terrorists to the detainment facility at Guantanamo Bay, Cuba. Nearly 70 percent of the casualties from Operation Iraqi Freedom came home on a C-141. This is the C-141B modification line.

The first flight of a production StarLifter took place in December 17, 1963, the 60th anniversary of the Wright brothers' first flight. It was slated for 10:35 a.m. that day, the same time at which the Wrights had flown. But a brake overheat light came on, prompting test pilot Leo Sullivan to remark, "Check it out, and [we'll] fly after lunch," which they, and he, did.

This shot of the first production C-141 during its maiden flight was snapped from a "chase" plane, probably a C-130 Hercules. The Marietta plant was rarely busier in its long history than it was in the mid-1960s with both the Vietnam War and Cold War at their heights. For example, the plant delivered 192 aircraft in 1966, including 58 C-130s, 9 L-100s, 22 JetStars, and 103 C-141As.

A C-141 StarLifter soars majestically over the Marietta plant in this shot from the 1960s. The sprawling plant dominates the foreground below, bounded to the left by what are now the CSX Railroad tracks. But the view beyond, toward north and east Cobb, is mostly fields and forest, with no sign yet of Interstate 75 or suburban sprawl.

Shortly after entering service, it was discovered the C-141 had an unusual problem as originally designed: it would run out of useable cargo area before hitting its weight limit. So to utilize its lifting capacity to its best advantage, the Nixon administration agreed to stretch each StarLifter by 23 feet. Here, one can see several C-141s in the process of being stretched.

The original version of the C-141 could carry up to 154 troops, or 123 fully equipped paratroopers. The stretched StarLifters could carry up to 205 soldiers, or 168 paratroopers. They also were roomy enough and powerful enough to transport vehicles; 13 standard-sized cargo pallets; or 104 litters of wounded servicemen.

The recently discovered remains from World War II of a fallen US service member are returned to this country aboard a C-141 at Hickam Air Force Base, Hawaii, as an honor guard awaits. A handful of StarLifters remained on active duty through 2006 and flew wounded servicemen and women out of Iraq and Afghanistan.

One civilian version of the C-141 was built, the L-300. But when no sales materialized, Lockheed donated the jet in the mid-1960s to the National Aeronautics and Space Administration, which used it as an airborne observatory. Seen here at the controls in 1982 are pilot Jim Martin (left) and copilot Ron Gerdes.

Lockheed's C-141 demonstrator plane, the L-300, was later acquired by NASA and modified to carry the Kuiper Airborne Observatory telescope. Its 45,000-foot ceiling allowed it to be above the visual effects caused by the Earth's water vapor, and its 6,000-mile range meant it could fly nearly anywhere on the planet to make its observations. The observatory was decommissioned in 1995.

Avionics technician Hap Arnold (left) stands by the Kuiper telescope, while crew chief Lloyd Dornier sits by the control panel in this photograph from October 1982. The L-300 crew in 1977 made the first sightings of the rings of Uranus and, a decade later, made the definitive identification of an atmosphere on Pluto, at the time still considered a planet. (*Marietta Daily Journal* photograph.)

This unusual-looking, big-nosed StarLifter is the Advanced Radar Test Bed, designed for airborne testing of radars and electronic countermeasures. It was later flown at the Air Force Flight Test Center at Edwards Air Force Base in California. The Marietta plant produced all 285 C-141s and modified 270 into the stretched C-141B. All C-141s are now retired, but they served their country with distinction for nearly four decades.

Not only did the Pentagon's fleet of cargo planes built in Marietta do yeoman work during the Vietnam War, it performed a poignant and gratifying service as that war drew near a close, which was ferrying home newly released US prisoners of war (POWs) from the hellish prisons in which they had been kept in Hanoi—some of them for up to seven years. In the picture above, one can see some of the ex-POWs as they make their way from a bus to a waiting C-141 StarLifter, marked with a large Red Cross on its tail. Shown below is a shot of the jubilant men taken aboard the C-141 as it prepares to take off from Hanoi.

The last C-141 in Air Force service was *Hanoi Taxi*, which had flown 40 just-released prisoners of war from Hanoi to Clark Air Base in the Philippines in Operation Homecoming at the end of the Vietnam War. The *Hanoi Taxi* was retired in 2006 after taking part in Hurricane Katrina rescue operations and giving the former POWs the chance for a last ride. In the picture at right, one can see the aircraft's maintenance crew chief paying his respects before the final flight, which ended at the National Museum of the US Air Force at Wright-Patterson Air Force Base in Dayton, Ohio, the hangars seen in this wintry picture below.

Despite the impressive size of the C-141 StarLifter, it nonetheless was not big enough to hold much of the equipment the Army needed. The solution chosen by the Air Force was a new aircraft, the C-5 Galaxy, made at Lockheed's Marietta plant and seen here at its rollout March 2, 1968. The Galaxy's 247-foot cargo area is longer than the first flight by the Wright brothers. Among the

many dignitaries who attended the rollout were Pres. Lyndon B. Johnson, First Lady Lady Bird Johnson, and Gov. Lester Maddox. Sadly, this C-5 caught fire and burned in October 1970 while undergoing maintenance at the plant, killing one worker and injuring another.

President Johnson (back to camera) quipped to the crowd at the rollout that he hoped someone had measured the width of the hangar doors to make sure the new plane could exit the plant. (They had.) Shaking the president's hand is Lockheed president Dan Haughton. At left, gazing admiringly at the president, is his wife, First Lady Lady Bird Johnson.

The weight of the C-5 Galaxy is distributed among the 28 wheels in its landing gear. Each is fitted with a Goodrich tire that can be deflated while in flight, depending on the conditions expected at the destination airfield. The tires have a combined weight of 4,214 pounds and hold 181 pounds of air when properly inflated.

This could almost pass for a children's jungle gym but is in fact the crew cabin—technically the fuselage cab top—of the first C-5B in the early stages of its construction. A close perusal will indicate the future location of the cockpit windows. Lockheed manufactured 50 of the C-5Bs to augment the Military Airlift Command fleet. A total of 81 C-5As and 50 C-5Bs were built.

C-5A and C-5B Galaxys were powered by four TF39 turbofan engines that were revolutionary when designed by General Electric in the 1960s for the C-5. Each of the four is 27 feet long and eight feet in diameter and weighs approximately four tons. Here, one can see the process it took to mount on a Galaxy's wing. The C-5M is receiving significantly more powerful and upgraded engines.

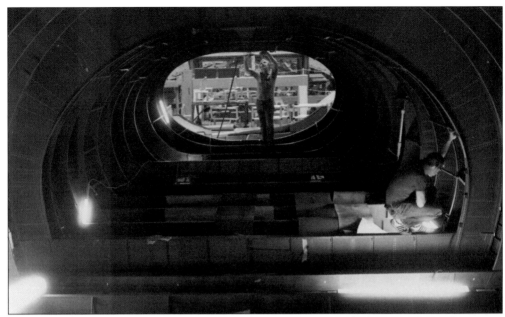

The inside of the C-5 actually consists of two decks—a lower one for heavy cargo and an upper one for passengers. It boasts seating for 73 people; although, like nearly every other military transport, passengers face the rear rather than forward for increased safety in case of an accident. For most of its career, the Galaxy usually carried a crew of eight, including three loadmasters. Crew complement has been reduced on the C-5 today, thanks to technology. This image shows the tail section under construction.

Paint is applied to a C-5B. Believe it or not, but just the paint on a C-5 weighs 2,600 pounds, or about the weight of an average private plane. As for fuel, a C-5 carries an amount sufficient to allow a typical US car to make 130 round-trips between New York City and Los Angeles.

More than 10,000 people gathered at the end of the runway in Marietta to watch the first flight of the C-5 Galaxy on June 30, 1968, with Leo Sullivan at the controls. Liftoff was at 7:47 a.m. Some waggishly suggested that was a sly dig at Boeing, which had unsuccessfully entered a military version of its planned 747 model in the competition to build the new cargo jet.

In a radical departure from previous cargo planes, the C-5 included both a cargo ramp in the tail and a nose visor that raises revealing a cargo ramp in the nose, meaning equipment can be driven in one end of the aircraft and out the other. This is the view looking through the wooden mock-up of a Galaxy's open nose toward its open tail.

The C-5 set numerous records for things like gross takeoff weight and size of cargo. In 1971, it proved it could carry two mobile scissors bridges, the Army's biggest piece of equipment, weighing in at more than 60 tons each. Here, in a picture from that era, one can see that the Galaxy mock-up has room to fit three jeeps and their drivers, abreast. And peeking out from further in is the muzzle from an artillery piece. The real aircraft demonstrates this capability daily.

The C-5, seen here, is big enough and powerful enough to haul not one but two 68-ton M1 Abrams battle tanks. The Galaxy fleet played a central role in Operation Nickel Grass, the emergency shipment of desperately needed supplies to Israel during the Yom Kippur War in 1973.

This leviathan of the sky pokes its nose out the hangar in Marietta. How big is the Galaxy? It is nearly 248 feet long (practically the length of a football field), with a wingspan of almost 223 feet. Equally impressive is its height, 65 feet. Empty Galaxys weigh 190,000 pounds. Their maximum takeoff weight is more than 840,000 pounds.

This C-5A arrived back in Marietta looking dirty and pretty much worse for the wear in this shot from the early 1980s. It was delivered to the Air Force in 1971 and stationed with the 60th Military Airlift Wing at Travis Air Force Base, California, and most likely was one of the first Galaxys returned to Marietta for the re-winging program.

It is up, up, and away for this Bensen Gyrocopter at an air show at Dulles International Airport in the early 1970s, as the C-5A at left almost seems to be laughing at the gyro's impertinence. The Bensen Company developed a series of small gyroscopes starting in the late 1950s. Bensens had a maximum speed of just 42 miles per hour but could climb to 12,500 feet.

Families and others stroll through the cavernous fuselage of a C-5 during one of the air shows held periodically at the Lockheed Martin-Dobbins complex. Such shows commonly draw upward of 100,000 people, attracted by the usual array of vintage military and civilian aircraft and the soaring acrobatics of the Navy's Blue Angels or the Air Force's Thunderbirds.

The C-5As developed wing cracks in the mid-1970s, meaning their cargo weight had to be restricted. The Pentagon eventually agreed to replace the wings on the C-5 fleet with completely new and much stronger wings. All told, 77 Galaxys were updated during the re-winging program. The picture at right shows a C-5 sans wings. The image above depicts a C-5 a few steps further along in the process; the new wings are in the process of being attached. In the foreground at the bottom can be seen the tip of one of the old wings that is still sporting the Air Force logo.

A new C-5B undergoes a pressurization check outside the west end of the main B-1 Building. Lockheed Martin has done a pressurization check on each of its new large aircraft (such as the C-130, C-141, C-5, and so on) as it rolls off the assembly line. The aim of this is to ensure that the aircraft is sealed correctly.

Here is how the first C-5B looked prior to its rollout at the L-10 Building in 1985. Its wings have just been installed but not its engines. Meanwhile, the final C-5A arrived in Marietta six months later for wing modification. It was redelivered to the Air Force at Dover Air Force Base in July 1987.

A pair of C-5s has their nose visors open. The C-5 was designed with a unique landing gear system that allows the parked aircraft to "kneel" or be lowered so that the floor of the cargo compartment is at the same height as the bed of a truck, making loading and unloading much easier and faster. Each could haul six Greyhound buses in its cargo compartment.

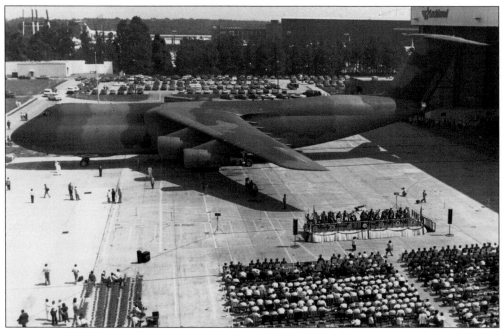

Rollout of the first production C-5B took place on July 12, 1985. The first C-5B flight took place that September in Marietta, and the first "B" was delivered to the Air Force three days after Christmas of that year. The Bs would prove crucial during US wars in the Persian Gulf in coming years. The entire airlift for Operation Desert Storm, for example, was equal to duplicating the Berlin Airlift every six weeks.

One of the first C-5B Galaxy transports lumbers into the sky from the Dobbins runway beside the plant. It included all the improvements and modifications made to that point on the C-5A, plus improved wings and updated avionics. The Marietta plant churned out 50 of the Bs between 1985 and 1989.

Here is a shot taken in the L-10 Building during wing installation for the Galaxy. Close examination shows one wing on each side in the process of being reattached with two other pairs of wings ready on either side of the plane to be reattached to the next plane in line. In the distance is another, parallel line of Galaxys undergoing the next step in the process.

The final C-5B manufactured in Marietta is seen here outside the maintenance hangar. The C-5 fleet did yeoman service during Operations Desert Shield and Storm and the later Operation Enduring Freedom in Afghanistan and Operation Iraqi Freedom in Iraq. Even though the C-5 fleet made up only 12 percent of the combined airlift fleet during the first Gulf War, it hauled 44 percent of all airlifted cargo to that area.

A C-5A Galaxy soars past Georgia's Stone Mountain in this shot from the early 1970s. C-5s have played vital roles in every US military conflict since Vietnam, including Desert Storm and the

wars in Afghanistan and Iraq. They also have excelled at humanitarian work, such as dealing
with the aftermaths of Hurricane Katrina and numerous floods and earthquakes.

Legendary Cobb County journalist Bill Kinney of the *Marietta Daily Journal* is at far left in this group posed on an F-84 Thunderjet at an air show at Dobbins in the 1950s. At far right is businessman Sig Tumlin, co-owner of Marietta Lumber. His nephew Steve "Thunder" Tumlin was elected mayor of Marietta in 2009. Those pictured are, from left to right, Kinney; Marietta First United Methodist's pastor, the Reverend Paul Turner; three unidentified individuals; and Tumlin. The F-84 was one of the earliest US fighter jets and compiled a distinguished record in the Korean War; although, according to pilots, it was not much fun to fly. Among their nicknames for the plane were "the Iron Crowbar," "the Lead Sled," "the Groundhog," and "the World's Fastest Tricycle." (Courtesy of Bill Kinney.)

Six

FRIENDS OF THE PLANT

With the glitz of the Cobb Galleria Centre and swank hotels still a decade or more away, the 25th anniversary of Lockheed's operation of the Marietta plant was celebrated in 1976 in the then new Cobb Civic Center. After many years in which nearly everything had gone right for Lockheed-Georgia, the plant was about to enter a decade of challenges and decreasing employment. (*Marietta Daily Journal* photograph.)

Dan Haughton (second from the left) makes a joke with Cobb Commission chairman Ernest Barrett (far right). Barrett served from 1964 to 1984 and is considered the most visionary person to have held that post. At left is Bob Sawyer. In dark glasses is Marietta insurance agent Harry Livingston Jr., a World War II B-17 pilot and prisoner of war. (*Marietta Daily Journal* photograph.)

Lockheed president Dan Haughton (left) leads US senator Richard B. Russell of Georgia on a tour of the plant in the 1950s. Russell, who was elected in 1933 and died in office in 1971, was one of the most quietly influential members of that body. He snared 15 military installations for Georgia during his 16 years as chairman of the Senate Armed Services Committee.

The Marietta plant has often been visited by celebrities, especially during the World War II and Korean War eras. Shown above is Ed Sullivan flanked in April 1954 by an array of showgirls. The newspaper gossip columnist had begun emceeing a variety show in the brand-new medium of television seven years earlier. It went on to be one of the longest running such shows in television history. In the picture below, hamming it up in front of a new B-47 at the plant, are, from left to right, test pilots Capt. Charles Estes, Maj. Paul Oliver, *Gone with the Wind* costars Cammie King and Ann Rutherford, test pilot Capt. Arleish Sampson, and actor (and future US senator from California) George Murphy. Among his movies were *A Girl, A Guy, and a Gob* and *Hold That Co-ed*.

Comedian Bob Hope (right) was no stranger to the plant. He first visited for a war bond rally during the Bell bomber era. He and his entourage often flew on Lockheed planes, particularly C-141s, as they toured far-flung military bases and war zones. Hope eventually bought a Marietta-built JetStar for personal use. Another well-known customer was billionaire Howard Hughes, who owned four JetStars that he kept under Hughes Company guards at the plant—but never flew.

Lockheed celebrated its 35th anniversary in Cobb County in 1986 and was feted by the Marietta Kiwanis Club at a banquet. From left to right are Lockheed-Georgia president Paul Frech, his successor Ken Cannestra, Georgia governor Joe Frank Harris, Kiwanis president Joe Cook, *Marietta Daily Journal* publisher Otis A. Brumby Jr., and retired Lockheed-Georgia president Larry Kitchen. (*Marietta Daily Journal* photograph.)

Editor Bill Kinney (left) of the *Marietta Daily Journal* was Lockheed's guest in 1958 on one of several brand-new Lockheed C-130 Hercules being delivered to customers in the Far East. He filed columns along the way at such then exotic locales as Kwajalein, Guam, Tokyo, and Seoul. He is pictured above in a white shirt with the two pilots as they exit the plane. He is also seen at right in the passenger compartment of a specially fitted Herk interviewing a Lockheed official en route. Kinney was still writing about Lockheed and its planes and people well into the 2000s. (Both, courtesy of Bill Kinney.)

In the early 1980s, the 94th Airlift Wing at Dobbins christened this C-130 *City of Marietta*. Pictured at the ceremony, from left to right, are Maj. Gen. Alan Sharp (USAF), Mayor Bob Flournoy Jr., Lockheed vice president and plant general manager Bob Ormsby, Gen. James McAdoo (USAF), US representative Larry McDonald, US senator Mack Mattingly (Republican, Georgia), and unidentified.

Sam Nunn, left, was elected to Richard Russell's US Senate seat in 1972 and served through 1996. Like his mentor Russell, Nunn chaired the Armed Services Committee and was key in obtaining funds for the C-141 stretch program. At center in this shot taken at the 25th anniversary in 1976 is Gov. George Busbee. At right is then state representative Joe Mack Wilson, chair of the House Ways and Means Committee and later mayor of Marietta. Close examination shows he is sporting a "Jimmy Carter for President" pin.

Max Cleland, in wheelchair, lost three limbs in a grenade explosion while serving as an Army officer in Vietnam. He later headed the US Veterans Administration during the Carter era and then was Georgia secretary of state. Cleland served in the US Senate from 1996 to 2002 and was a consistent supporter of Lockheed-Georgia products. He is seen here while touring the plant as senator.

US senator Johnny Isakson (Republican, Georgia) was one of many officials on the runway beside the Lockheed Plant in 2005 to mark the completion of the 2,300th copy of the C-130 Hercules, a Marine Corps KC-130J tanker. Isakson, like all but one or two Georgians on Capitol Hill for the past half century, has been a strong advocate for the Lockheed Plant. (Courtesy of Lockheed.)

The B-1 Building is well on its way to completion in this photograph of this building taken in late 1942 or early 1943. The view is looking due east toward Blackjack Mountain at right. A dozen or so workers are barely visible on the roof. And just to the left of the plant's base is a parked locomotive. One of the reasons for the plant's location was that it was on the main line of the Norfolk Southern Railway, making it convenient for shipping in construction materials and aircraft components. The plant is the biggest building in Cobb County by far, at 3.8 million square feet, equivalent to 76 football fields. Also, with the possible exception of one or two steeples in Marietta, it was the tallest at 4.5 stories. It cost $52 million to build the plant. In contrast, it cost $22 million to replace the B-1 air-conditioning unit in 1996. The following are some other numbers: the B-1 Building boasts 42 miles of overhead crane track, 44,919 sprinkler heads and, originally, 72,704 fluorescent lights (38 miles worth). They were replaced with 1,100 sodium vapor lights, which are now being replaced by a like number of energy-efficient compact fluorescent lights.

Seven

THE PLANT

The north side of the B-1 Building is the site of a parking lot nearly as big as the plant, seen here during the mid-1950s. In an era when there were no giant shopping malls and no mammoth stadiums in Georgia, this was probably the largest parking lot that most employees had ever seen.

The B-2 Building (at center of picture) housed the plant's executive offices and was connected to the main B-1 assembly building by an enclosed breezeway. The B-2 Building was erected hastily early during World War II and was meant only as a semipermanent structure. Nearing the end of its useful life, it became more and more outmoded; half of it was demolished in 2007.

Here is an overhead view of the L-10 Building—at one time the world's largest free-span cantilever building (all the support for the roof is on the roof)—under construction in 1967. It houses the design, engineering, and program management for the C-5 Galaxy. Although most of the Lockheed operation is in the government-owned Air Force Plant 6 Industrial Area, with the massive B-1 Building as its nucleus, Lockheed owns considerable acreage, including the L-10 site, on the south side of the runway along Atlanta Road.

Starting with the C-141 StarLifter in 1960 and continuing through the F-22 Raptor in the 2000s, most of the planes built by Lockheed in Marietta were designed at the plant. That not only helped ensure its viability and importance to corporate headquarters but also had the beneficial side effect of creating thousands of well-paying jobs and attracting many highly educated people to Marietta through the years. Seen are plant engineers at work in the 1980s, with a C-5 Galaxy model overhead.

Gridlocked scenes, like this, called by workers "the Marietta 500," were common outside the Marietta plant when tens of thousands of vehicles converged for each shift change. Employment at the plant peaked at 28,000 during World War II and again at 32,945 in late September 1969 as the C-5A program was in full swing. This shot was taken along South Cobb Drive looking east toward the present site of Cobb County's school bus barn.

Now rusting derelicts, these once-shiny C-130s were manufactured at the plant in 1972 for the Libyan government, which paid $70 million for a total of eight Herks. But before they could be delivered, dictator Moammar Gadhafi had taken power and had begun supporting international terrorism and trying to subvert moderate Arab and African governments. That caused Washington to clamp an embargo on the sale of military weapons to Libya, preventing the delivery of the Herks. The eight planes sat for years between the plant and adjacent Dobbins Air Reserve Base, but now have been moved to a remote corner of the property.

The Low Speed Wind Tunnel at Marietta opened in 1967. To celebrate the tunnel reaching the 100,000-test-hour milestone in 2005, technicians hung an F-22 wind tunnel model on the "sting," the boom that airplane models are tested on, over a former NASCAR racing car to symbolize the tunnel's two main test subjects, aircraft and cars. In the automotive world, Ford and NASCAR have been the tunnel's top commercial customers.

Lockheed's wind tunnel also boasts this low-speed testing compartment. A future transport design similar to a Boeing 707 is being tested by worker Debi Saliga in this shot snapped in 1989. Among the aircraft whose aerodynamics were tested there were models of the C-5, C-130, and F-35 Joint Strike Fighter.

In the mid-1990s, the plant unveiled the C-130J, an almost complete upgrade of the original Herk, boasting better avionics, engine, and hauling capacity, as well as shorter takeoff and landing ability. Lockheed sent the Marietta-built C-130J on an around-the-world tour in 1998 to showcase it to future clients. Among its many stops were several in the Middle East, including this one in Egypt, where the Herk has been called "the Flying Camel." Another stop was in South Korea, where a pilot from the Republic of Korea Air Force, or RoKAF, exclaimed in surprise during his test flight, "It drives like a Porsche!" Nearly every letter in the alphabet has been employed at times to identify variants of the Herk. Prefixes have included AC, CC, DC, EC, GC, HC, JC, KC, LC, MC, NC, RC, SC, TC, VC, WC, and the YC-130. Suffixes have included C-130A, AEH, B, CL, D, E, F, G, H, J, K, MP, N, (N), P, Q, R, (RR), S, T, U, V, and X.

Eight

THE "J"

Each of the C-130J's four engines is propelled by six-blade composite propellers manufactured by Dowty, a Cheltenham, England–based company formed as Rotol Airscrews in 1937 by Rolls-Royce. Rotol went on to manufacture propellers for several of Great Britain's most famous fighters of World War II, including the Hawker Hurricane and the Supermarine Spitfire. (*Marietta Daily Journal* photograph.)

A C-130 Hercules nears completion in the B-1 Building. Having been in production longer than any US military aircraft in history, the C-130 has been the Lockheed Plant's most dependable program since the 1950s. The Hercules is a cash cow, bringing in significant income for nearly six decades to Lockheed and Lockheed Martin.

Six C-130Js are seen here on the assembly line steadily making their way toward the exit door of the B-1 Building. The rate of production of the Hercules has varied greatly through the years, depending on demand. The peak year was 1957, with 140 aircraft. The lowest was 1997, when only two were delivered as the plant converted from the H to the J model. The rate was three per month for many years in the 1980s and 1990s. This went down to 12 but came back up starting in 2008, going from 16 aircraft in 2009 up to 24 in 2010, with 36 scheduled for 2011.

Above, the first C-130J is delivered to the 146th Airlift Wing at Channel Islands Air National Guard Base in California. Beside it is the Modular Airborne Fire Fighting System 2, called MAFFS 2, used for dumping flame retardant and water on forest fires. In less than five seconds, the C-130J can drop 3,000 gallons of retardant weighing 28,000 pounds, enough to cover an area a quarter-mile long and 60 feet wide. The plane can later be refilled in less than 12 minutes. The retardant is a phosphate-based fertilizer mixed with water and orange dye. It is corrosive to aircraft, so a rust inhibitor is also included. The retardant either smothers a fire or coats the vegetation to prevent it from catching fire and thus provides a firebreak. Below, a Channel Islands C-130J is shown in action, dumping water on a training mission in 2009.

The C-130J has set numerous records for speed, altitude, and payload. The Hercules, with its "cutaway" tail section, was designed to be extremely effective at Short Take Off and Landing (STOL) flying. Test pilots Lyle Schaefer and Arlen Rens set 29 world records on April 14, 1996, in a WC-130J, as seen in this John Rossino photograph.

Employees gather around the 200th C-130J Hercules produced at the plant in this overhead shot from fall 2010. The Hercules went into production in 1955 and has been rolling off the flight line ever since. It is flown not only by the US military but also by air forces from all over the world. This aircraft, an HC-130J personnel recovery tanker, is also the 1,500th C-130 built for the US military. (Courtesy of Lockheed.)

The Herk is designed to operate on all kinds of unusual surfaces, even snow and ice. The C-130D model was the first variant to employ the largest ski system ever used on an aircraft. The plane can take off and land with either the wheeled landing gear or the skis, which weigh a ton each and are retracted during flight. A ski-equipped LC-130H (like this one), with temperatures near its operating limits, landed in Antarctica in 1999 to rescue a scientist afflicted with breast cancer.

This is a Lockheed WC-130 Weatherbird manufactured at the Marietta plant. It is one of several versions of the Herk "storm-chaser" that has been in production since 1962 and is modified to allow it to penetrate tropical disturbances, storms, hurricanes, and typhoons. The Weatherbirds can stay aloft nearly 18 hours cruising at 300 miles per hour and are assigned to the 53rd Weather Reconnaissance Squadron, the "Hurricane Hunters," at Keesler Air Force Base, Mississippi.

The C-130J, like predecessor Herks, is designed to carry troops and their equipment to airfields near the front lines that might come under fire. The J's ability to take off from short runways and land after a steep descent has made it a key player in the wars in Afghanistan and Iraq, seen here. Air Force and Marine Herks flew more than 2,650 sorties during Operation Iraqi Freedom.

Sales to foreign countries have helped the Hercules maintain its status as the plant's bread-and-butter product since the 1950s. These nearly complete C-130Js are part of a package of six purchased by the Indian Air Force. Lockheed also provides training for the aircrew and maintenance technicians. Other countries flying the C-130J include Australia, Canada, Denmark, Italy, Norway, and the United Kingdom, which was the J's first foreign customer. More than a dozen countries are flying J models or have them on order.

An early model C-130 Hercules was seen flying overhead in the early 1960s at Kitty Hawk, North Carolina, on an earlier page of this book. Here, one can see the newest version of the Herk, an HC-130J, with its distinctive six-bladed propellers, as it soars over the Kitty Hawk Memorial. This photograph was taken in 2003 at the 100th anniversary of the Wright brothers' first powered flight. This aircraft belongs to the US Coast Guard and is based at Coast Guard Air Station Elizabeth City, North Carolina. A member of the Life-Saving Service, a predecessor to the Coast Guard, took the famous photograph of Orville Wright on that first flight in 1903.

Italy has been a strong customer of the C-130 Hercules for more than 35 years, and that relationship has continued in the "J" era. That country became one of the first foreign buyers of the C-130J in 1997, and since then Italian crews have compiled well over 75,000 flight hours in them. One of those Js is seen here overflying the Leaning Tower of Pisa, just under the aircraft's right inboard propeller.

The Lockheed Martin F-22 Raptor, simply put, is acknowledged as the most dominant fighter jet ever built. It was conceived in the early 1980s as an unmatched blend of super-agility and stealth and boasts a top speed in excess of Mach 2—although the exact speed remains classified. A stealth fighter designed to be difficult to see with the naked eye and all but invisible on radar, the Raptor also is capable of identifying and destroying targets well beyond the visual range of the pilot. The Air Force originally planned to acquire 750 copies of the Raptor, but with the end of the Cold War, and due to the F-22's flyaway cost of about $140 million per plane (in 2009 dollars), Congress and the Pentagon bought only 187.

Nine

THE PLANT TODAY AND TOMORROW

The first flight of the production F-22 took place September 7, 1997, from the Lockheed-Dobbins runway in Marietta with Lockheed chief test pilot Paul Metz at the controls. Even though the F-22 has been flying since 1997, it still is widely considered to have no match in aerial combat. (*Marietta Daily Journal* photograph.)

Lockheed vice president and plant manager Ken Cannestra was all smiles moments after watching the live announcement, via closed-circuit television in Marietta on April 23, 1991, that the Pentagon had awarded Lockheed the huge contract to build the F-22. The news culminated an intense, high-stakes, five-year demonstration/validation competition between Lockheed and Northrop-McDonnell Douglas. Cannestra later was promoted to head of Lockheed Aeronautical Systems and retired in 1996.

Engineer Micky Blackwell was a key figure in the development of the F-22—first at the famed Skunk Works in California and later in Marietta, where he served as plant manager. He went on to become president of Lockheed Aeronautical Systems Company and then president of Lockheed Martin's Aeronautic Sector before retiring in 1999 after 31 years with the company.

The F-22 system program officer, or SPO director, speaks to a crowd of engineers at the plant in the early 1990s. At rear is one of the prototype YF-22 aircraft that had been assembled by hand at Lockheed's plant in California. It later had its wings removed and was flown aboard a Marietta-built C-5 Galaxy to Georgia, where it was used primarily as an engineering mock-up.

The F-22 final assembly takes place at the plant, but many of its thousands of components are manufactured elsewhere and then shipped to Marietta by rail or truck. The plant's Technical Support Center (TSC) allows the company, working with Air Force representatives, to keep track of the status of every Raptor at every operational base. One of the main things the TSC watches is the level of parts already on hand or in stock at bases. (Lockheed Martin)

A MISTAKE
COVERED UP MAY
COST THE LIFE OF
A BRAVE PILOT

EXIT

THROUGH THESE DOORS PASS THE
MOST AWESOME FIGHTERS IN THE WORLD

Pilots flying the YF-22 prototype used the radio call sign "Lightning" during test flights in 1990, and it was widely thought that the F-22 would have that as its official nickname. However, it was formally christened "Raptor" by the Air Force in 1997. Lockheed built the 200,000-square-foot L-22 Building south of the runway in the early 1990s to house those working on the F-22 program; however, these pictures were snapped in the B-1 assembly building. On the wall are two signs. The first cautions, "A mistake covered up may cost the life of a brave pilot." The other, located below the huge flag, reads, "Through these doors pass the most awesome fighters in the world." Workers at the Marietta plant had crafted 174 copies of the Raptor by the end of 2010, with the remaining 13 to come off the line in 2011.

The Lockheed Martin–led international team was selected in 2001 to build the F-35 Lightning II. Also known as the Joint Strike Fighter, it is a stealth, supersonic, multi-role, multi-variant fighter for the United States and its allies. It will be flown by the Air Force, Navy, and Marines and in three versions—conventional takeoff and landing version, short takeoff and vertical landing option, and a carrier-based variant. The Marietta plant is building the center fuselage for the F-35. Above, one can see the first landing at Lockheed-Dobbins. The F-35 looks quite similar to the F-22 to the layman. At right, plant workers are setting up the tooling for the F-35. It is a far cry from some of the machines pictured in first chapter of this book.

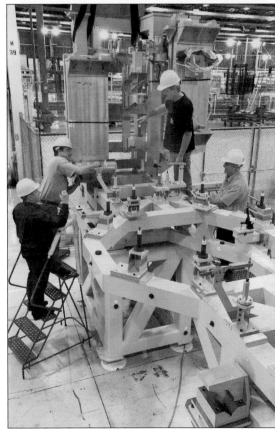

Lee Rhyant, the son of a Georgia sharecropper, was a newcomer to Lockheed Martin and the plant when he was named vice president and plant general manager in 2000. But he will go down as one of the plant's most accomplished and popular leaders. Former vice president of production at Rolls-Royce Aerospace in Indianapolis, Indiana, Rhyant helmed the Marietta plant until his retirement in early 2011, the longest tenure of any of its managers.

More than 750 Orions have been manufactured by Lockheed since 1959, but only eight by the Marietta plant, which were purchased by South Korea's navy. The plant now is building replacement wings for the P-3. That process begins with the wings in an upright position, as seen here.

Previously serving as vice president of human resources for one of Lockheed Martin Corporation's four business units, Shan Cooper took over from Rhyant in early 2011. She is no stranger to Marietta, having spent two years heading human resources. Unlike her predecessors, she has no background in engineering, but like them, she is prepared to face the challenge of keeping the plant and its aircraft competitive. Here, she is taking her first ride aboard a C-130.

A C-5 Galaxy soars upward with Mount Rainier in the background in this shot taken at the semiannual Airlift Rodeo held at McChord Air Force Base near Tacoma, Washington, in 2007. A Galaxy set a world record at the event in 1989 by air-dropping four M551 Sheridan light tanks and 73 paratroopers from the 82nd Airborne Division.

Air Force and Lockheed Martin officials are silhouetted against the first C-5M Super Galaxy, *Spirit of Global Reach*, at the delivery ceremony at Dover Air Force Base in Delaware in 2009. The Super Galaxy has new avionics, upgraded engines, and more than 70 other improvements. These modifications are designed to improve reliability and keep the C-5 flying for 40 years. The C-5M is able to haul more cargo both faster and further plus land and take off from shorter runways.

A C-5M Super Galaxy takes off from Dobbins Air Reserve Base. The Air Force initiated another upgrade program in the 2000s to ensure the C-5's capability into the 2040s. It includes enhanced avionics and upgrades to the engines to improve reliability. When complete, those C-5s are redesignated as C-5M and are known as Super Galaxys. A September 2009 test run by a joint Air Force and Lockheed Martin flight crew resulted in 41 world aeronautical records set in just one flight.

How big is a C-5M? It is very likely the biggest airplane one will ever see, as this photograph makes abundantly clear. Those who played a part in its development are gathered for this photograph at the September 2010 delivery ceremony of the first production Super Galaxy. It is a smaller crowd than the one shown early in this book, from when the plant reopened in 1951, but it is a reminder of how many strides there have been in aviation since then—and it is an indication of the vital role that the Lockheed Martin Plant in Marietta has had in so many of them.

Discover Thousands of Local History Books Featuring Millions of Vintage Images

Arcadia Publishing, the leading local history publisher in the United States, is committed to making history accessible and meaningful through publishing books that celebrate and preserve the heritage of America's people and places.

Find more books like this at
www.arcadiapublishing.com

Search for your hometown history, your old stomping grounds, and even your favorite sports team.